Simple fixes for your car

How to do small jobs yourself and save money

Also from Veloce Publishing

This publication has been produced on behalf of RAC by Veloce Publishing Ltd. The views and the opinions expressed by the author are entirley his own, and do not necessarily reflect those of RAC. New automotive technology is constantly emerging; the information in this book reflects the status quo at the date of publication.

www.rac.co.uk
www.veloce.co.uk

First published in October 2012 by Veloce Publishing Limited, Veloce House, Parkway Farm Business Park, Middle Farm Way, Poundbury, Dorchester, Dorset, DT1 3AR, England. Fax 01305 250479/e-mail info@veloce.co.uk/web www.veloce.co.uk or www.velocebooks.com.

ISBN: 978-1-845845-18-6 UPC: 6-36847-04518-0

Simple fixes for your car

How to do small jobs yourself and save money

Carl Collins

Contents

Introduction

Who this book is for

Car owners with little or no mechanical skills who want to keep their motoring costs down and the car on the road instead of in the mechanic's garage.

Why buy this book?
• Because there are many things that can go wrong with your car that don't need a mechanic to put right.
• Because it shows you how to keep your car on the road, and save you money on parts and time.
• Because you don't need any mechanical skill to use it.

It can often be more convenient and less costly to perform your own simple fixes, rather than take your car to the garage. The book is written in plain English, with simple step-by-step instructions, supported by many illustrations.

All of the products used in this book are cost-effective, and readily available from most car parts shops, as well as online.

What's not in this book
This is not another book showing you how to check and top-up your car's engine oil level, engine coolant or windscreen washer bottle: there are books out there already that will tell you how do do these jobs, including books in this series.

What is in this book
Without any mechanical skill or specialist tools, this handbook will tell you how to identify and change fuses, repair windscreen chips and cracks, fix broken mirrors, remove paintwork scratches, repair exhausts, and fix many more simple faults.

Important information & about the author

Important information

• The vehicle manufacturer's handbook (referred to as 'car user manual' throughout this book) should take precedence over the information contained within this book.
• The guidance in this book is generic, so, whilst your car and its components may look a little different to the featured project cars and their components, the actions described can still be performed in essentially the same way.
• All bolts, nuts and screws are turned anti-clockwise to undo, unless stated otherwise.
• Always use the correct size tools (spanners, sockets, screwdrivers, etc) or you risk damaging parts of the car and yourself.

About the author

For many years Carl Collins has been providing technical content for his automotive help website: www.carbasics.co.uk.

His engineering background, training experience and passion for all things automotive have equipped him to write highly detailed, yet easy-to-follow car DIY articles. Since 2006, his website has helped hundreds of thousands of car owners save money, and keep their cars on the road.

As a result of this success, Carl is now in the process of writing a number of books on automotive subjects.

one

Electrical faults

Fuses

All car electrics will have a fuse controlling the power going to them, so if, say, the rear window heater stops working, there's a good chance that the fuse has blown.

Car fuses blow for many reasons, and often replacing them will get things working again. Think of them the way you would a household electrical plug: if a fuse blows on an appliance at home, you simply change the fuse, and you're up and working again; the same usually applies to your car.

Where is my car's fusebox?

Fuseboxes are typically found in one of two places – and sometimes both: inside the car under the dashboard, and in the engine bay.

Under the dashboard it will be in one of the footwells; your car user manual should locate it for you. It will be behind a panel, so pull out the panel and have a look behind it. An engine bay fusebox may be on the left or right, and probably toward the back, away from the headlights. It will have a plastic cover over the top to keep the contents clean, and will contain numbered fuses of different colours, similar in purpose to household plug fuses: different value fuses for different applications.

Fusebox, here located in engine bay.

Fusebox, here located behind a panel under the dashboard.

Pulling out the fuses for inspection. There's usually a plastic tool for this.

How to identify a blown fuse

Automotive fuses are designed so that you can quickly check whether they have blown. Many can be checked without removing them from the fusebox, but others will have to come out.

The fuses pull out using finger and thumb and just push back in. Only check one fuse at a time (see images) and ensure fuse goes back into the correct slot.

Fuse tips

• Check that your fusebox has plenty of spares; replenish from your local car parts store. They are very cheap, and with today's modern cars being so heavily reliant on electrical components, spare fuses are essential

• If you have a fuse that repeatedly blows, this indicates an electrical fault: get it checked out by an auto-electrician as soon as possible

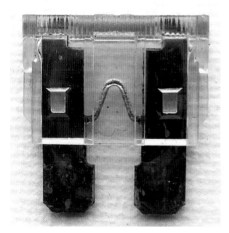

Sound fuse: centre track is intact. (Courtesy carbasics.co.uk)

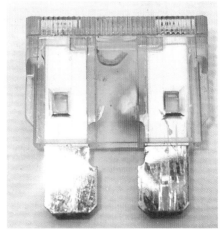

Blown fuse: centre track is broken; fuse needs replacing.

Rear window heater not working

If only a few tracks on your rear heater are working this will be because there may be a break in one or more of the heating tracks on the window.

It is quite common for the tracks on the heater to become damaged, especially if you have been transporting large items in the rear of your car. If these have rubbed on the rear window whilst driving, it may have resulted in a break in the tracks.

Rear window heater connectors & heater fuse

If the rear window heater is not working at all, the heater connectors and the fuse should be checked.

Rear heater connectors

Usually two push-on (spade) connectors supply power to the heater, one on each side of the window. Check that both connectors are attached and fixed firmly.

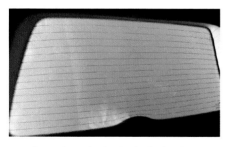

Inspect rear heater tracks for breaks.

If one or both have broken off, re-attach using a suitable conductive glue (also referred to as wire glue). You cannot use ordinary glue as it will not conduct electricity, and the rear heater will not work.

Heater fuse

Check whether the rear heater fuse has blown (see "Where is my fusebox?"

for your fusebox location and how to change a blown fuse). If your rear heater switch normally illuminates to show when it is on, it's probable that the fuse has blown if it doesn't light up.

Inspecting heater tracks

Inspect the tracks on the rear windscreen by looking for any gaps: best done by either looking through the rear window from the back seat of the car or, if your car has a tailgate, opening this and looking through it upward toward the sky. Damaged tracks should be evident as they will let more light through.

Repairing heater tracks

A number of kits are available with which to mend rear heater tracks, and these normally include conductive paint, a paint brush, and masking tape. The conductive paint bridges the gap in the track and allows it to work again.

The repair kits usually include full instructions; here's a brief guide:

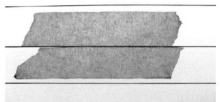

Preparing heater tracks for repair using masking tape.

- Identify the broken tracks as described.
- Ensure that the ignition is off.
- Fix masking tape top and bottom of the damaged track.
- Using the brush, apply the conductive paint over the broken area, ensuring that the paint overlaps the track each side of the break.
- Repeat for all broken areas.

• Allow paint to dry and remove masking tape.

You should now be able to test your repair the next time that the rear window mists up.

Rear heater repair tips
• Ensure that the conductive paint overlaps the track each side of the break.
• If you already have masking tape and a fine brush, just buy conductive paint instead of a complete kit. It's probably best to source this type of product online: it's also used in electronics for repairing circuit boards.
• You may find it easier to source conductive glue or wire glue online as it may not be available from your local car parts shop.
• If, after performing the checks and repairs in this chapter, the rear window heater is still not working, you will have no option but to take your car to an auto-electrician to identify and repair the fault.

Electric windows not working
If you experience a problem with your car's electric windows, there are a few quick checks that you can do initially.

If none of the windows work the most likely cause is a blown fuse. See "Fuses," for your fusebox location and how to identify and change a blown fuse.

If just one of the windows has stopped working, it's most likely due to a fault with that specific window motor or the wiring going to it. To find out if it's something as simple as a loose plug or a broken wire, you will need to remove the inside door panel.

Chapter 8 gives guidance on how to remove door panels but, if this is not a job you wish to undertake yourself, it is recommended that you take your car to a garage to investigate the problem.

Central locking not working
If the central locking works fine with the doorkey but not with the remote key fob, first assume that the battery inside the key fob needs replacing.

If you have a new battery in the key fob and the central locking still only works using the key, assume that either the key fob has a fault or there is a fault with the remote receiver within the car. Either way, it is recommended that you take the car to an auto electrician for a more thorough inspection.

If neither the remote key fob nor the door key will operate the central locking, the first thing to check is whether the central locking fuse has blown. See "Fuses," for the fusebox location and how to identify and change a blown fuse.

If the fuse has not blown there is a problem elsewhere in the central locking system that will need to be investigated by an auto-electrician.

Replacing the remote key fob battery
Changing the battery is pretty easy, and all you need is a flat-bladed screwdriver and a new battery. The battery will most likely be the small, round type, commonly referred to as a 'watch' or 'button' battery.

The battery type will be marked on the battery itself, for example "CR1620 3v." These batteries can be purchased online and are readily available from most supermarkets.

Changing a key fob battery
• Take the key fob off the keyring and lay it on a flat surface.

Remote control key fob.

• Carefully split the casing in two to reveal the battery.

Note which way the battery goes in because, if you put the new one in the wrong way, it won't work and the fob may not even go back together again properly. Put all the parts in place and press the casing together.

Open the key fob slowly, being careful not to lose any pieces it may contain, such as small springs, and noting where everything fits.

Exterior lights not working

• Some fobs are held together using small screws. Remove these first and then using a flat-bladed screwdriver, gently prise open the plastic casing where the two halves join (see your car's handbook for exact procedure).

If a set of lights are not working the fault may not be with the lights but with the fuses that control the lighting circuits. Your car user's manual should contain a section that advises which fuses control which components. Identify which

Main: Opening remote key fob using flat-bladed screwdriver. Inset: Remote key fob button battery.

Typical interior light. (Courtesy carbasics.co.uk)

numbered fuses control the lights that are not working and inspect them. See "Fuses" for the fusebox location and how to identify and change a blown fuse.

For information on how to change your exterior light bulbs, see chapter 5.

Horn not working

If the horn stops working, there could be a number of reasons why, the most common being that the fuse has blown. This is a simple check and may solve the problem very quickly. See Fuses, above, for your fusebox location and how to identify and change a blown fuse. Your car's user manual should tell you which fuse controls the horn.

If the fuse has blown change it for a new one of the same value. Test the horn, and if still not working, have an auto-electrician or mechanic investigate the problem.

One other common reason for horn failure is that the wiring connectors may have come off or become corroded. It's unlikely the user manual will tell you where to locate the horn (sometimes they can be quite inaccessible) but you could enquire online whether anyone

can provide any pointers. This is worth a try as it may just be a case of re-attaching the connector that powers the horn. If not, you will need to take the car to a local garage which should be able to help.

Interior light not working

The interior light(s) should come on when you open the car doors, or when they are activated by the relevant switch. This section covers the most common interior light faults, and how to fix them easily without the need for an auto-electrician, but first establish that the interior light is actually switched to the correct position.

The most common reason for failure is either the light bulb or the fuse has blown.

Check to see if your car's other interior lights (such as the map light) are working and, if not, this indicates that it is most likely a blown fuse that is at fault. See "Fuses," for the fusebox location, and how to identify and change a blown fuse.

Changing interior light bulb
If you have determined that it is the bulb at fault, it is a very quick job to change

Releasing interior light lens with flat-bladed screwdriver (methods will vary).

Interior light bulb: W5W type.

Interior light bulb: dome type.

it. Most interior lights are easy to change as the clear lens is designed to unclip with the aid of a flat-bladed screwdriver (if uncertain see your car's handbook for exact procedure).

The accompanying picture shows a typical interior light bulb. They simply push into place and the clear cover can be pressed back on; the job is done.

Check if the interior light now works. If it doesn't, the fault is elsewhere and will require further investigation (but see following two sections also). If the wiring is securely attached and there are no blown fuses, you will need to enlist the help of an auto-electrician.

Interior light controlled by pin-switches

On older vehicles it could be that the door pin switch has failed, and on more modern cars there could a fault with the electronic module that operates the interior lights.

Check whether your car has pin-switches by opening its doors and looking around the door opening (see image opposite), usually in the bottom corner furthest from the door hinge (not on the actual door).

These can normally be undone by either removing the fixing screw of by unscrewing the outerplastic retaining collar (anti-clockwise). With the pin-switch removed from the bodywork, check for signs of rust or corrosion. Also, ensure the wiring is pushed securely onto the back of the pin-switch.

Check for signs of rust or corrosion on the pin-switch screw, and around the screwhole, as this may prevent the switch from working. Ensure the wiring is pushed securely onto the back of the pin-switch; also check the connector for signs of corrosion.

If your car does not use door pin-switches, proceed to the next section covering electronic modules.

Interior lights controlled by electronic modules

Many modern vehicles have electronic modules that control many electrical items, such as central locking, interior lighting, exterior lights, etc. Manufacturers give these components various names – Citroën/Peugeot (BSI: Body Systems Interface); Renault (UCH: Unite Central Habitacle); Ford (GEM: Generic Electronic Module); Audi/VW/Skoda (CCM: Comfort Control Module).

Fault finding on these modules is not a simple matter, and way beyond the scope of this book. However, it may be just that the control module needs a reset in order to get it working again. It may be possible to perform a reset yourself, and you should look online for possible solutions. Alternatively, the car will need to be taken to a garage or main dealer with specialist equipment to perform the reset.

If, after you have performed the reset, the interior lights are still not working, it is recommended that you investigate the matter further online or take your car to an auto-electrician.

Interior light pin switch inside door opening.

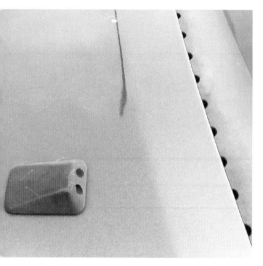

Windscreen washer jets mounted on bonnet.

Windscreen wipers not working

As usual, the first thing to check with inoperable wipers is the fuse. See "Fuses," for your fusebox location and how to identify and change a blown fuse.

If the fuse has blown, replace it with one of the same value and retest the wipers.

If the wipers still do not work, enlist the help of an auto-electrician or mechanic.

If the windscreen wiper fuse keeps blowing, this indicates that there is a fault with the wiper motor or wiper mechanism which will require the attention of a mechanic.

Warning – Never operate the wipers when someone is adjusting or inspecting the wiper motor or wiper mechanism.

Windscreen washers not working

If you operate your windscreen washers and nothing happens, there are a number of causes that you can check for.

Firstly, with the engine turned off and the ignition still on, activate the washer jets and listen for a whirr to check that the pump is operating.

If you can hear the pump working but there's no water spraying onto the windscreen, check that your washer bottle has washer fluid in it. If the washer bottle is empty, refill it.

If you can hear the pump working and there is washer fluid in your washer bottle, it may be that the washer jets are blocked: see chapter 3, "Unblocking washer jets," for guidance.

If there is still no water spraying onto the windscreen after cleaning out the jets, check for blockages in the pipes that feed the water to the washer jets, usually located on the underside of the bonnet. These usually just pull off connectors to allow you to check for blockages by either blowing through them or feeding wire inside them.

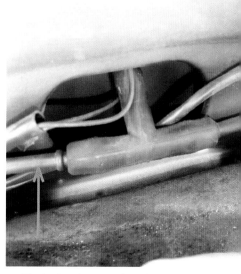

Washer jet pipes run along the underside of the bonnet.

two
Coolant leaks

In this chapter water leaks are referred to as coolant leaks, as your engine cooling system should contain a mixture of part anti-freeze/summer coolant and part water – not 100 per cent water.

Spotting and rectifying coolant leaks early can help to prevent major breakdowns and save you a small fortune: a coolant leak may not necessarily mean an expensive trip to the garage or the need for a breakdown service. This chapter will cover a number of repairs you can undertake yourself using products from your local car parts shop, or even from the nearest fuel filling station.

Repairing a radiator coolant leak

If you have identified that you have a leak coming from the radiator, you can effect a repair yourself using one of the many radiator 'stop-leak' additives that are readily available. These are designed to locate small leaks in your cooling system and seal them permanently. These additives are not expensive and are very easy to use.

How do they work?
The liquid is poured into the cooling system's expansion tank, and mixes with the coolant already in the system. The repair works on a 'coolant-to-air' basis, the liquid becoming solid at the point where the coolant is leaking from the system under pressure, and coming into contact with the air. Modern and good quality additives will only become solid when they come into contact with the air. The heat from the engine cooling system also contributes to the repair process.

Most reputable products also have anti-corrosion and lubricating properties that will further assist the cooling system, and not clog up or leave sludge deposits. The following are reputable and effective products: RAC Stop-Weld,

Add leak repair via the expansion tank, as you would anti-freeze.

Holts RadWeld, Wynn's Radiator Stop Leak, Bars Leaks, and Kalimex K-Seal.

How to use stop-leak additive

Warning – do not work on leaks until the engine coolant has cooled sufficiently as you are at risk from scalding: this includes removing the coolant filler cap too soon.

Most modern cars do not have radiator caps, so the following details how to get the leak repair liquid into the coolant system via the expansion tank.

Before you start, make sure that you have a supply of water/coolant to top-up the cooling system – perhaps in a watering can or plastic bottle. The leak will continue for a while after the repair until the additive has circulated and located the leak.

Make sure that you read and follow the instructions on the product label exactly. The following is a brief explanation for your guidance:

• Pour the correct amount of stop-leak additive into the expansion tank or radiator.
• Start the engine and observe the leak.
• The engine will pump the additive around the cooling system until it plugs the leak.

After the leak has been repaired, top-up the coolant level.

• You should see the leak reducing progressively, and then stopping.
• Unless stated otherwise in the instructions, once the leak has stopped you can turn off the engine and top-up the coolant system as necessary.

How long will this repair last?
If the product you use is high quality, and the manufacturer a reputable one, it is entirely possible that the repair will be permanent.

Radiator leak tips
• Adding stop-leak additives can also seal leaks in the heater matrix (part of the in-car heater). If you have water leaking inside your car, and feel that it is from the heater matrix, following the foregoing procedure may rectify this problem also
• Using stop-leak additives may also repair a hole in a coolant hose, but because of the flexible nature of the hose, and the effects of engine vibration and movement, a better repair would be made using a self-amalgamating repair

tape, as described in the next section "Repairing a coolant hose leak."
• After identifying and repairing a leak, always keep a close eye on the engine coolant level. If a radiator leak re-appears, you can always use more additive. However, if a leak consistently re-occurs, it's possible that the repair is beyond the scope of a stop-leak additive, and a replacement part will be required.

Repairing a coolant hose leak

If you have identified a coolant leak coming from a hole or split in a coolant hose, you can effect a temporary repair until you are able to replace the part.

Most car parts shops will have "emergency hose repair tape" that is designed to seal a leak to allow the car to continue to be used. Please note that this is not a long-term fix, and the leaking hose should be replaced as soon as possible.

It's not recommended that you drive your car to collect the repair part when it is leaking coolant in case of overheating and engine failure. However, if you must drive the car, ensure that you take a large plastic bottle of water to top-up the engine cooling system. You must also keep a very close eye on the dashboard warning lights and stop immediately if any come on. Running an engine when low on coolant can be catastrophic – and very costly!

Make sure that the repair tape you purchase is specifically designed for use on cars, and that it can withstand very high and very low temperatures.

How to use hose repair tape

Warning – do not work on leaks until the engine coolant has cooled sufficiently as you are at risk from scalding: this includes removing the coolant filler cap too soon.

In order to make the best possible repair, remove all dirt and oil from around the pipe split. If you do not clean and dry the area thoroughly, the repair tape will not stick to the pipe, and the coolant will continue to leak out.

Ensure you follow the instructions exactly on the product you have purchased. Don't cut any corners, and take time to make sure the area is thoroughly clean. An extra few minutes of cleaning at the start can avoid having to do the repair all over again.

One of the best ways of cleaning a hose is to use WD-40. Spray some onto a rag and clean the hose with this.

Once the area is completely clean and dry, you can start to apply the repair tape.

Do not apply the repair tape just over the hole: start one to two inches to the left or right of it, and work across and past it by the same margin, ensuring that the hole is in the centre of the repair, and you have used enough tape before and after it.

Overlap the tape as you apply it:

usually, a 50 per cent overlap will give a good repair.

Once the repair has been done, check the coolant level before you start the engine.

When you do start the engine, it is important to check that the repair has been effective: the most likely reason why it won't have worked is that the area was not cleaned sufficiently.

How does it work?

Most of these repair tapes are 'self-amalgamating': as they warm, the layers will merge, forming a water-tight seal. So, once you have started the engine and confirmed there are no leaks, it's a good idea to keep the engine running for a while so that, as coolant temperature rises, it will warm the repair tape, and start the amalgamation process.

Once the leaking hose has been repaired satisfactorily, the car should be fine to drive until a replacement hose is fitted. Get the faulty hose replaced as soon as possible to avoid more serious damage to the car.

How long will this repair last?

A good and clean repair can last quite some time, but should never be considered a permanent fix. The hose has already failed once, after all, and will probably fail again, perhaps in a different place.

Hose repair tips

• If you have had to perform a repair on a coolant hose, make sure that you check the coolant level as often as possible. A poor repair could cost you a new engine if your vehicle overheats.
• After you have performed the repair and warmed the engine for a short while, apply a little hand pressure around the tape as this will help the amalgamation process.

three

Windows and windscreen

Without good visibility you cannot drive safely. This chapter covers everything from adjusting your windscreen washer jets to repairing a chipped windscreen.

Cleaning a smeary or streaky windscreen

A smeary windscreen may not automatically mean that you need to replace the wiper blades, as there are many reasons why you could be getting smears. For example, the wax cycle on a car wash could be responsible, or even the wax in the cleaner you use to wash your car at home.

To remedy this situation, begin by cleaning the outside of your windscreen and the wiper blades. Neat distilled/white vinegar is an excellent solution to use to clean your windscreen and wipers, and is easily and cheaply sourced from your local supermarket.

Use a micro fibre or lint-free cloth,

Neat distilled/white vinegar is ideal for cleaning windscreens and wiper blades.

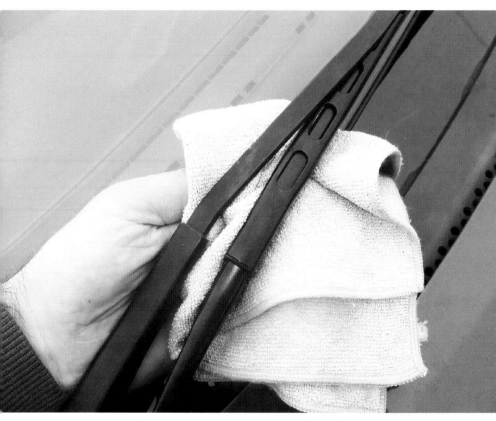

Cleaning windscreen wipers using distilled/white vinegar.

apply the cleaner to the cloth, not the windscreen. Thoroughly clean the entire windscreen, lifting the wipers from the screen to do so: give these a thorough wipe, also.

If any residue remains after the windscreen is dry, buff this off with a soft, clean cloth.

Windscreen cleaning tips
• If, after giving your windscreen a good clean, you are still unhappy with visibility, it may be necessary to replace the wiper blades. (See "Wiper blade replacement").
• Consider applying a rain-repellent, such as Rain-X, to your clean screen,

as this will help keep it really clean, and water will disperse more easily, further aiding visibility. (See "Applying window/rain treatment").

Wiper blade cleaning, repair and replacement

How to repair a split wiper blade
Wiper blades often split, causing part of the cleaning tip to detach from the rest of the blade. When this happens, the wiper blade will no longer clean the windscreen properly, and will need to be replaced as soon as possible (see "Wiper blade replacement").

A split windscreen wiper blade will deteriorate very quickly. (Courtesy carbasics.co.uk)

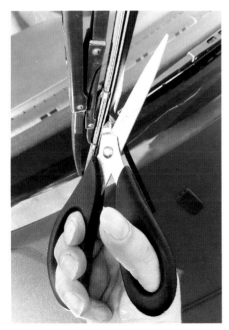

Cut off the damaged part of the wiper blade.

As a very short-term simple fix, cut off the loose piece of wiper blade with a pair of scissors. If you don't do this, it will continue to split further every time you use the wipers and, eventually, the cleaning surface of the wiper blade will detach from the body, resulting in seriously impeded visibility.

Wiper blade replacement

Your car's wiper blades won't last forever, and motoring organisations such as the RAC recommend changing wiper blades every 12 months. If you are noticing smears and streaks when using your windscreen wipers, it's probably time to get them changed.

Don't take your car to the garage to get it done; it's a 5-minute job, and you should really notice an improvement in visibility. You don't need any tools, and you can buy replacement blades from your local car spares shop or online.

A standard wiper blade, wiper arm and plastic clip. (Courtesy carbasics.co.uk)

Which are the right wiper blades for my car?

Wiper blades are most commonly sold by length, usually measured in inches. If you buy your replacement wiper blades online, you should be able to select your vehicle make and model and the website will tell you what size your car uses. Always check these recommendations against your own measurements, though.

The most common type of wiper consists of a wiper arm, a plastic clip and the wiper blade itself.

The plastic clip slides into the 'J' shape at the end of the wiper arm and holds the wiper blade in place

These are called standard wiper blades, and the following guide will tell you how to change them.

How to change standard wiper blades

• Lift the wiper arm from the windscreen, and rotate until it is rubber-side up (a T-shape).
• The plastic fastener holding the wiper blade to the upright arm sits inside the J-shaped hook at the end of the arm.
• Depress the plastic clip and, at the same time, pull the wiper blade down the arm toward the bonnet.
• You should now be able to remove the wiper blade from the wiper arm.
• Take your new wiper blade and check the plastic clip is the same as the one on the old blade. Replacement wiper blades normally come with a number of interchangeable clips, but if there are no suitable clips you will have to use the one from your old blade (these should just pull off).
• With the rubber of the new wiper blade facing upward, feed the 'J' end of the arm through the blade next to the plastic clip, and hook it over the top.
• Pulling the wiper blade upward should lock the plastic clip into the end of the 'J' on the wiper arm.
• Now fold the wiper blade and arm back down slowly so that it rests on the windscreen.
• Your new wiper blade is now fitted; follow the same procedure for the other blade.

Push-button-type wiper blades

Some vehicles are fitted with push-button-type wiper blades, and these are really easy to change. Where the wiper arm joins the wiper blade is a plastic clip which has a button on it: pressing this will allow you to remove the wiper blade. Once done, simply push the new wiper blade onto the arm and it will clip into place.

Wiper blade tips

• If the clip holding the wiper blade

Depress the plastic clip to release the wiper blade.

With the clip depressed, pull the blade and clip down the arm to detach.

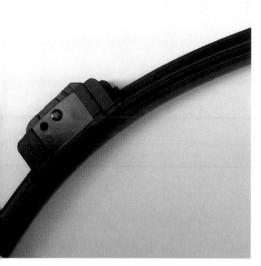

Beam-style wiper blade: consider upgrading to these if you don't already have them.

A windscreen chip can quickly develop into a crack if not repaired.

Typical windscreen chip repair kit, available from most auto spares shops.

to the wiper arm is stiff, and will not easily release, spray it with WD-40 to free it, but don't get any lubricant on the windscreen or bodywork.
• Measure all of the wiper blades that need changing, as many modern cars have differently-sized driver- and passenger-side blades.
• Consider upgrading from standard wiper blades to what are now referred to as 'flat blade,' 'beam' or 'aero' style blades. These modern blades are designed to give much better full-width contact with the windscreen, and are also reported to reduce wind noise.

Fixing a chipped windscreen

A chipped windscreen does not necessarily mean that a replacement is required, and repairing a fixed windscreen is cheaper and easier than you might think. The windscreen repair

kit used in this chapter was purchased online, and can be used for multiple cracks or chips. It comes with complete instructions, and everything you need is in the kit.

Remember that you do not need any mechanical skills to perform this repair, and it could save you a lot of time, money, and hassle.

How does it work?
With most windscreen repair kits, a special liquid is injected into the crack or chip, which, when dried/cured, will have repaired the damage and restored

Typical contents of windscreen chip repair kit.
(Courtesy carbasics.co.uk)

Windscreen chip repair kit applied to screen
ready for repair.

windscreen integrity and strength.

Using a chip repair kit
Ensure that you read the instructions
carefully before you start work.
    The following is a brief guide to how
to use a kit:

• Begin by thoroughly cleaning
the window. For advice on this,
see "Cleaning a smeary or streaky
windscreen."
• Attach the support frame to the
windscreen with the suckers, ensuring
the crack or chip is directly in the centre.
• Screw the barrel into the support
frame so that the end touches the
crack/chip.
• Pour a small amount of the repair
liquid into the barrel.
• Slowly screw the plunger into the end

of the barrel: this will force the repair
liquid into the crack/chip.
• Remove the plunger, barrel and
support frame from the windscreen.
• Put one drop of the repair liquid onto
the top of the crack/chip, and then
place the curing film over the top.
• Allow the repair to dry/cure as per the
manufacturer's instructions.
• Once the repair is dried/cured, scrape
away any excess resin using the blade
supplied, and the repair is complete.

Chip repair kit tips
• Most windscreen repair kits need to
be used in sunlight, as the materials
used can only dry/cure when in UV light.
Most kits need only around five minutes
of UV/sunlight to dry/cure.
• Most windscreen repair kits cannot be
used at night or in wet weather.

Applying rain treatment

This is the same kind of product that motorcycllsts use on their helmet visors to aid visibility whilst riding in wet weather. A very fine, smooth coating is applied to the windscreen, and helps to disperse water more easily and readily. Another advantage is that it will help your windscreen stay cleaner for longer, because less water on the windscreen makes it more difficult for dirt to adhere to the glass.

You will also find that removing snow, frost or ice from a treated windscreen is a lot easier to do.

How does it work?
By sealing the microscopic holes in the windscreen glass that rain water and dirt like to stick to.

One treatment can last for up to three months, and it is not washed away by water or car shampoo, although, over time, use of the wiper blades will necessitate another application.

How to apply windscreen rain treatments
• Firstly, give your windscreen a good clean, (see "Cleaning a smeary or streaky windscreen").
• Read and follow the instructions provided by the manufacturer.
• Apply the treatment to a soft, lint-free or micro fibre cloth.
• Wipe firmly onto the windscreen in a small circular overlapping motion, working first on one side of the screen and then the other.
• Let the treatment dry to a haze, and buff off with another clean, lint-free cloth, ensuring the entire window is covered.

Re-apply the treatment when nessersary, depending on how often the wipers have been used.

Windscreen rain treatment tips
• Before you give your windscreen a good clean, consider washing the entire car. This will remove any dirt from around the edges of the windows, which may get wiped back onto the window when applying the treatment, and impair its effectiveness.
• You can also use the treatment on side/rear windows, and door mirrors to help improve visibility.

Applying anti-fog treatment

If you are having problems with interior windscreen condensation and misting, especially in cold weather, consider using an anti-fog treatment.

These are designed to minimise the effects of interior condensation on your windscreen, and improve visibility. They cannot prevent condensation forming, but will alter how it builds up on the glass so that your vision is less impaired, and moisture can be cleared away faster.

How does it work?
Anti-fog treatments (also referred to as anti-mist) work by reducing surface tension, helping the moisture disperse across the windscreen instead of beading together in droplets (which prevent you from seeing through the windscreen). Allowing them to instead disperse into a fine surface film will improve visibility.

How to apply anti-fog treatment
Ensure you follow the product instructions exactly. The following is a guide to application:

• Dependent on the product you purchase, it may come with its own applicator cloth. If not, you can use paper towel or a lint-free cloth.

• Clean your windscreen with a suitable glass cleaner or white vinegar, and a lint-free or micro fibre cloth.
• Remove any residue.
• Spray or pour a little treatment onto the towel/cloth.
• Wipe onto the entire windscreen in a circular, overlapping motion, re-applying small amounts of treatment to the cloth as necessary.
• Do not touch the windscreen after the treatment has been applied.

Re-apply the treatment regularly as per the manufacturer's instructions (usually every 1-2 weeks).

Anti-fog treatment tips
• To avoid smears when applying the liquid, do not apply too much at a time. It's better to apply in small amounts and build up as required.
• You can buy anti-fog wipes for use on the inside of your windscreen instead of applying an anti-fog treatment.

Adjusting windscreen washer jets

If, when you activate your windscreen washers, the water jets don't go where you want them to (eg: over the roof instead of on the screen), they require adjustment.

If your windscreen washer jets are the pinhole type, they can be adjusted quite easily with just a thin pin/needle using the method that follows.

Certain models can't be adjusted using this method, so you will need to refer to the user manual to find out how to alter water jet angles.

Some vehicles have just two jets, one each side of the bonnet, whilst others have four (two on each side). However many jets there are, each can usually be adjusted independently of the others.

Adjusting a washer jet with a needle. (Courtesy carbasics.co.uk)

Getting correct adjustment of the washer jets is a case of trial and error, and you may have to adjust and retest them a few times before you are happy.
• First job is to fill the windscreen washer bottle so that you have plenty of water to play with as you adjust the jets.
• Spray the water jets and check where they contact the windscreen.
• Insert a pin/needle into the washer jets and lever the jet to alter position. Ideally, the spray should contact the screen just above the centre.
• Once you have adjusted one jet, retest its trajectory with another spray.
• Keep re-adjusting the jets until you are happy with the spray positions.
• Repeat the process for the remaining jets.

Unblocking washer jets

If you have noticed that one or more of your windscreen washer jets is not working or is not working very well, it's likely that there's a blockage inside the jet.

It can be quite easy to clear any blockage by inserting a thin pin or needle into the jet. Test the washer jet again to check the blockage is cleared.

Keep your windscreen washer fluid bottle topped-up when adjusting and checking the jets.

four

Battery faults

Battery-related problems are the most common cause of breakdowns and vehicle faults, and this chapter will tell you about simple fixes that you can do yourself, thus saving you time and money.

Car memory

It is important to note that disconnecting your car battery may result in lost information, such as your radio security code, so ensure you know these details before you disconnect the battery so that the information can be re-entered when the battery is reconnected. Check your radio user manual or other radio documentation for the code, without which your radio will not work, and you will have to remove the radio from the dashboard in order to access the serial number, and pay a company to provide you with the correct code (usually four digits). Your main dealer can usually provide radio codes, however there are companies online that can provide the same service at a fraction of the cost.

If you do not know your radio security code, an affordable and hassle-free alternative to losing the use of your radio, or having to pay to acquire the code is a 'memory saver' or 'radio code keeper.'

These products can be purchased from most large car accessory shops as well as online, and will enable your electrical system to retain radio codes, clock settings, ECU settings, and other electrical details. They are designed to plug into the cigarette lighter of your car and provide power to your electrical system in the absence of the battery's power.

Many 'memory savers' also come with crocodile clips for attaching to the battery cables when the battery terminals have to be removed from the car battery and you cannot use the cigarette lighter.

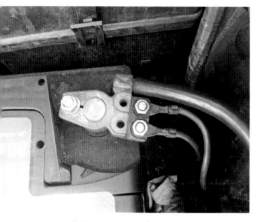

Bolt-on-type car battery terminal.
(Courtesy carbasics.co.uk)

Tightening battery terminals

If you are experiencing car starting troubles, always check first that the battery terminals are in place and secure: these connect the car to the battery, and must be firmly in place to allow power to your car. Terminals can vibrate loose over time, and then cause problems with starting the car.

The battery terminals may have a cover over them to keep them free from

Checking battery terminal for movement.
(Courtesy carbasics.co.uk)

dirt, so remove this in order to check terminal security (the covers usually just clip off or fold out of the way).

Checking terminals warning
• Always work with the engine off, and never touch both battery terminals at the same time.
• Do the battery terminals appear loose? Check this by trying to rotate each of them around the battery posts: there should be no movement at all when the terminals are clamped to the battery posts.
• **Warning!** Do not let tools touch the positive battery terminal and any other metal part of the car at the same time.

Types of battery terminals
The two most common types of battery terminal are bolt-on and quick-release.

Tightening bolt-on terminal
To tighten these you should require only a spanner or socket (usually 8mm or 10mm).

• Use the spanner to loosen the battery terminal (usually anti-clockwise).
• Now ensure that the terminal is pushed as far down to the bottom of the battery post as possible. It may help to twist it slightly as you push down so as to get good contact between the parts.
• Use the spanner to tighten the battery terminal (usually clockwise), making sure it remains firmly down on the battery post.
• Check again for any rotational movement.

Bolt-on battery terminal tip
• Do not over-tighten the battery terminal as this may cause damage. The terminal need only be tight enough to prevent it rotating on the post.

Tightening bolt-on-type battery terminal with a spanner.

Quick-release-type battery terminal.

Tightening quick-release terminals
• Operate the lever that opens the battery terminal.
• Ensure that the terminal is pushed as far down to the bottom of the battery post as possible. It may help to twist it slightly as you push down so as to get good contact between the components.
• Operate the lever again to tighten the battery terminal onto the post.
• Check again for any rotational movement.
• If there is movement, check that the quick-release lever is in the fully closed position.

Quick-release battery terminal tip
• Ensure the terminal is pushed as far down the battery post as it will go before you tighten it. Battery terminal posts are tapered, meaning that they are thicker at the bottom than at the top.

Charging a 'flat' (discharged) battery

Before commencing any work on your car's battery, ensure that you have read the important information at the start of this chapter relating to radio security codes and electrical memory.

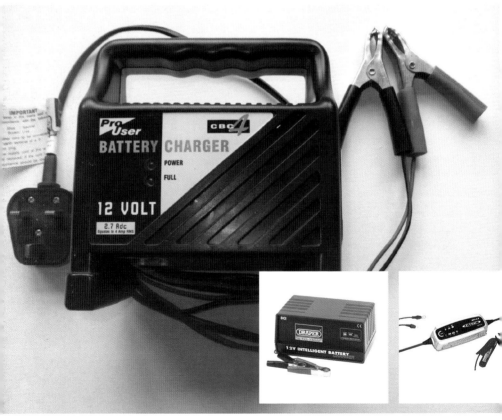

Main: Car battery charger. (Courtesy carbasics.co.uk)
Inset: A range of battery chargers are available direct from RAC - http://www.racshop.co.uk.

Car batteries lose their charge and 'go flat' for lots of reasons: here are just a few:

- The battery is getting old.
- The car has been standing unused for a while.
- The alternator is not charging.
- Lights, etc, have been left on.
- Very cold weather.

Car battery chargers are inexpensive to buy and easy to use, and can save you a lot of hassle and money (for a new battery).

How to use a battery charger

Batteries are extremely heavy, so be careful that you don't injure yourself when moving yours.

Before you begin charging the battery, you may need to check its electrolyte level, so read the section "How to check battery levels," before starting work.

To charge the battery, you will need a battery charger, a suitably-sized spanner or socket, and about eight hours' charging time.

If your car is parked close enough

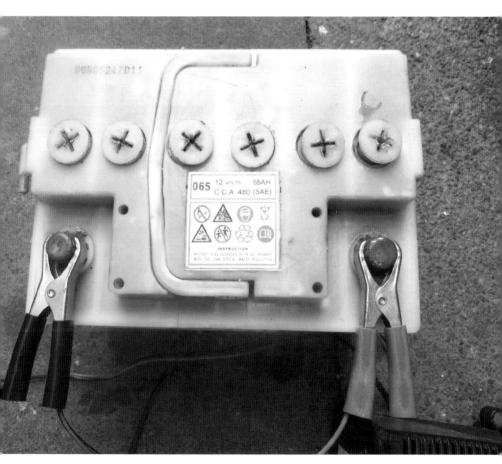

Battery charger connected to battery with cell plugs loosened.

to your house or in a garage, you can leave the battery in the car whilst it is charging, although you must disconnect both positive and negative battery terminals before you commence charging. **Warning!** Always disconnect the negative terminal first.

If you have to take the battery out of the car, locate it in a safe area with plenty of ventilation, and away from children, pets, naked flames and sparks.

In both instances, refer to the section "Changing a car battery," for guidance on how to safely release the battery cables.

As stated earlier, do not proceed to charge your car battery until you have read the section "How to check battery electrolyte levels."

Make sure you have read the manufacturer's instructions that come with the battery charger.

If your car battery has cell plugs on top, ensure that they are loosened or removed. Gases will be released during charging, and these will need to vent to atmosphere.

With the battery charger unplugged, connect the red charger clip to the positive terminal of the battery, and the black clip to the negative terminal.

Plug the battery charger into the mains and switch it on.

Leave the battery charging overnight. In the morning the charger should indicate that the battery is fully charged.

Switch off and unplug the charger, remove the charger clips from the battery (negative first and then positive), and refit the cell plugs before moving the battery.

Refit the battery to the car: see section "Changing a car battery," for guidance.

With the battery fully charged, the car should now start. If it still does not start, it could be that the battery is faulty

or there is a problem elsewhere with the vehicle. At this point it is recommended that you seek the advice of an auto-electrician or look online for help. Although this book does give guidance on how to fit a new car battery, without further investigation you could end up buying a new battery unnecessarily, and not resolving the problem.

Battery charging tips

• if you have not followed the guidance in the section "How to check battery electrolyte levels," your battery charger may tell you that the battery is fully charged when it isn't. This may be because there is insufficient electrolyte (the liquid inside the battery that allows electricity to flow from one plate to another – between positive and negative electrodes in each battery cell) which will cause the charger to give a false reading
• If the battery keeps going flat, there is possibly something wrong with the battery or the alternator, or something else is draining the power. Investigate further online or seek the advice of an auto-electrician.

How to check battery electrolyte levels

Checking battery electrolyte levels is an important first step before other fixes, such as charging the battery or using a battery booster.

You do not need to disconnect the car battery in order to check levels: this a quick job which could extend battery life.

Types of car battery

There are essentially two types of battery: sealed (or maintenance-free), and unsealed.

Usually, a label on the battery will identify which type of battery it is. If the

Maintenance-free car battery with health indicator: no topping-up required.

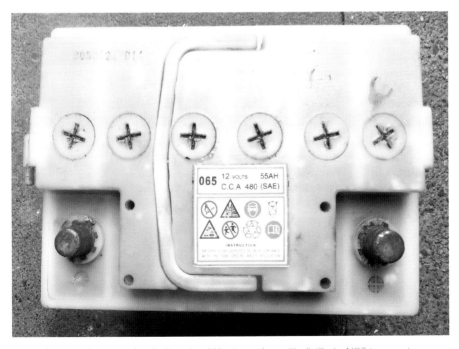

A non-maintenance-free battery should be topped up with distilled – NOT tap – water.

battery is sealed (maintenance-free), you do not need to be concerned about electrolyte levels.

To check battery electrolyte levels you will need a torch, a flat screwdriver, and distilled or de-ionised water (NOT ordinary tap water as this will destroy the battery cells). If the cells inside your battery are not filled with electrolyte, they will become damaged and a new battery will be necessary.

Topping-up battery levels
With the screwdriver, either remove the press-on strip or individual round cell plugs so that you can see inside each cell.

Many batteries have fill levels in the cell, but, if yours doesn't, ensure that the metal plates inside are completely covered with electrolyte. Pour in the distilled water slowly, and do not overfill the cells as you will not easily be able to remove excess. Fill to the indicated level or to just cover the metal plates.

Only use distilled or de-ionised water to top-up batteries.

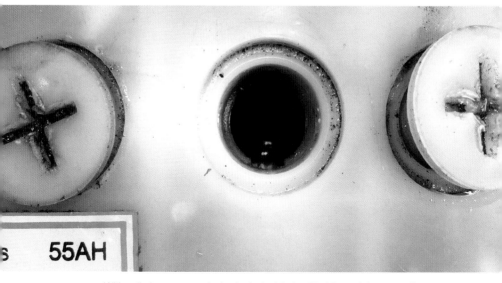

With cell plugs removed, check electrolyte level inside each battery cell.

Once each cell has been filled, you can refit the cell plugs.

That's your battery levels checked; you can now move on to other battery-related fixes.

Changing a car battery

Before commencing any work on your car battery, ensure that you have read the important information at the beginning of this chapter relating to radio security codes and electrical memory.

Advantages of changing the battery yourself

Changing a car battery is not difficult to do, and doing the job yourself could save a lot of time and money. You can shop around for a new battery and get the best deal, then change it at a time that suits your schedule, and not that of the mechanic.

The importance of the right battery

In order to ensure longevity from a new battery, firstly determine which is the right type for your car. For example, diesel engines require a more powerful battery to start them than do smaller petrol engine vehicles because of how diesel engines work. Assuming that your current battery is correct for the car, it should have a label on it displaying the necessary details. If not, check your car's handbook or look online for more detailed information.

When do I need to change my car's battery?

If the frequency of problems, such as

Battery label: 480 amps, 55 ampere hours.

difficulty starting in cold weather, is increasing, it's probably time to get a replacement battery.

Before buying a new battery you might want to consider having a look at the section "How to check battery electrolyte levels, above. Topping-up levels and recharging the battery may postpone the need to buy a replacement.

Removing the old battery

If you look down the side of the battery you should see a clamping set-up that holds the base of the battery in place. Another common type of battery holder consists of a strap or brace that runs across the top of the battery.

As detailed earlier, there are normally only two types of battery terminal: bolt-on and quick-release.

If your car has bolt-on terminals,

you will need an appropriately-sized spanner or socket to unfasten it (usually 10mm).

If your car has quick-release terminals, you won't need any additional tools to remove these. Note that some vehicles will use both types of battery terminal.

Disconnecting and removing the battery

* Batteries are extremely heavy, so be careful that you don't injure yourself when moving yours.
* To prevent injury, never let your hands or any tools touch both battery terminals at the same time.
* Label the battery leads before removing them as they are sometimes the same colour or it's difficult to see which is postivie and which is negative.
* Unclamp the negative (- black) battery

Typical battery clamp arrangement for securing battery base to car.

terminal first, and lift the terminal from the battery post.
• Ensure that the black wire you have just removed is located away from the battery; tucked out of the way so that it cannot come into contact with the battery.
• Unclamp the positive (+ red) battery terminal from the battery post, and also tuck that out of the way.
• With both of the wires safely out of the way, now unfasten the battery clamp or strap/brace using the appropriately-sized spanner or socket.
The battery should now be free to be lifted out of the engine bay.

Fitting the new battery
A reversal of the removal process, the following is a brief guide:

• Put the battery in place, ensuring that the terminals are the correct way round. If you put the battery in the wrong way round, the wires will probably not reach the battery posts: most cars are designed this way so that you cannot fit the battery the wrong way around, but ensure that the red battery wire goes to the positive (+) battery post, and the black wire to the negative post.
• Now double-check that the battery is in the right way round. Connecting a battery incorrectly can cause very expensive damage to your car's electrics, so check it at least twice.
• Attach the positive battery terminal to the battery first and tighten it (first ensuring that the terminal is pushed well down onto the battery post).
• Attach the negative battery terminal to the battery and tighten it (first ensuring that the terminal is pushed well down onto the battery post).

Unfastening battery clamp with spanner.

Lift lever to unfasten quick-release battery terminal. (Courtesy carbasics.co.uk)

Removing bolt-on battery terminal: unfasten with spanner.

• Refit the battery clamp or strap/brace, and check that the battery is secure.

Battery changing tips
• **Warning!** Always remove the negative battery cable first to avoid causing a short circuit, and possibly damaging your vehicle electrics
• After the new battery has been fitted and tested, smear petroleum jelly onto the battery terminals to prevent corrosion
• If you leave your car without any battery power for longer than 20-30 minutes, you are at risk of losing the radio code, which will necessitate re-entry of the code. Make a note of the radio code before you disconnect the battery (refer to your user manual for details of how to retrieve the code, and read the section on 'memory savers' at the beginning of this chapter.
• Your local landfill site should accept your old battery without charge. Parts of it will be recycled in a safe and controlled manner. Do not simply dump your old battery somewhere as it can present a danger to people, animals and the environment.

Using a battery booster

Most of us will have suffered from a flat battery at some stage in our driving experience, and a very useful item that all households should own – especially if there is more than one car in the family – is a battery booster.

What is a battery booster or jump starter?
This piece of equipment contains a large battery that can be charged at home using a normal socket. Via its red and black leads, power from the booster's battery is passed to your car's battery to start the car.

Advantages of owning a battery booster
Always having a battery booster fully charged at home means that you should always be able to start a car with a flat battery and get it back on the road. Some boosters also have a torch on them, and some a tyre pressure tester and inflator, too.

How to use a battery booster
Always follow the manufacturer's instructions relating to charging the battery booster and using it on your car. Make sure your battery booster is fully charged before you use it.

Always read the manufacturer's instructions before you use the equipment. You will not need to disconnect the car battery. The following is a brief guide to using a battery booster:

• Ensure that the ignition is switched off.
• If the booster cables are long enough, place the booster on the ground. If

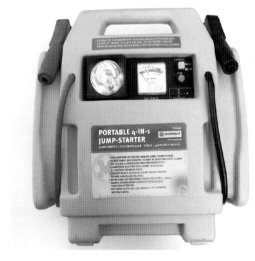

Battery booster for starting a car with a flat battery. (Courtesy carbasics.co.uk)

not, rest it in a safe location away from moving car parts, where it will not fall off when the engine is started.

• First, connect the red cable to the positive (+) terminal of the battery and, second, the black cable to the negative (-) terminal of the battery.

• Now start the car as you would normally.

• It is not recommended that any cables are disconnected from the battery with the engine running. This can damage sensitive electronics on the car.

• Allow the engine to run for a few minutes, then switch it off and disconnect the battery booster, negative first and positive second.

• The vehicle should now be able to be started under its own battery power.

Battery booster tips

• When you take your car for a drive to charge the battery, take the battery booster with you just in case you need to restart the car again.

• If you are having to use a battery booster on a regular basis, there is an underlying fault with your car. You could need a replacement battery (see "When do I need to change my battery," above) or alternator. It is recommended that you read all of the sections in this chapter, and take your car to an auto-electrician to have the fault investigated.

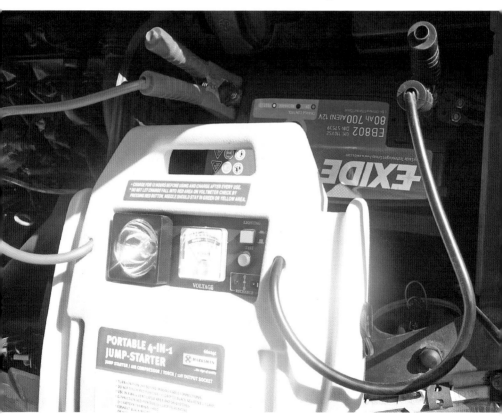

Battery booster connected to car battery. (Courtesy carbasics.co.uk)

five
Lights/indicators

Cracked light lenses repair

Headlights, indicators, and rear lights are vulnerable to damage, but it may not be necessary to replace the complete unit if this happens.

You can make simple repairs to lights using lens repair tape which is cheap, easy to use, and available in colours of clear, red and amber.

A damaged rear light can be repaired instead of replaced.

Lens repair tape should prevent the damage from getting worse, allow your car to pass any necessary inspections, and keep it road-legal.

How to use lense repair tape
Follow the manufacturer's instructions exactly, but the following is a brief guide:
* Clean and dry the damaged lens using a lint-free or micro fibre cloth. Failure to do this properly can mean the repair tape peeling off over time.
* Cut a suitably-sized piece of repair tape and apply to the damaged area.
* Press down on the repair tape with your fingers, ensuring it sticks firmly to the light lens, and smooth away any bubbles or creases.

Restoring scratched or dulled headlights lenses

The plastic outer lenses of headlights can become cloudy or dull over time due to exposure to UV light. There are

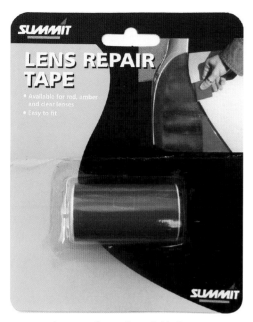

Lens repair tape is available from most auto spares shops.

Lens repair tape applied to damaged rear light.

Headlight restorer falls into two categories: those that are applied by hand with a cloth and those that come in kit form and require the use of an electric drill to apply the liquid/paste.

Essentially, both cut through any oxidisation and debris, and polish the surface so that it is clear again.

The hand-applied method is much the cheaper of the two, but will never provide the same level of repair as the kit version, no matter how much time you spend polishing the headlight lenses. Choose the product type that you are comfortable with using, and ensure you follow the manufacturer's instructions.

Do not use bodywork scratch remover liquids on your lights: although mildly abrasive, they are not designed for use on plastics or glass.

You will not be able to remove a deep scratch or gouge from a plastic-lensed headlight by merely polishing it.

Changing exterior light bulbs

Note: It can be possible to upgrade your headlight bulbs by installing higher wattage versions than those originally fitted by the manufacturer, but be aware that higher wattage means higher temperatures. Most headlight units are made from plastic, so the use of higher wattage bulbs could cause them to become misshapen because of the extra heat. It's best to contact the vehicle manufacturer for advice if you are interested in upgrading.

HID headlight bulbs
Some manufacturers are now fitting as standard, 'Xenon'/HID (High intensity discharge) lighting systems (your handbook will tell you if your car is so equipped). HID units provide up to 300 per cent more light than some ordinary bulbs and consume less electricity.

products that you can use at home to get the lenses looking like new again, and they are also ideal for removing small scratches and scuffs.

Unlike ordinary bulbs, HID bulbs do not have a regular metal filament. They work on the principle of a spark of around 20,000 volts being used to activate the gas and metal salts contained in a tube to form a plasma, then a continuous supply of around 85 volts is required to keep the arc lit.

If you have these bulbs fitted, they generally give a warning when they are about to fail, as they may start to flicker.

It is not recommended that you change these bulbs yourself, mainly because the high voltages required to operate them represent a real hazard if the lights are not completely isolated electrically. HID bulbs are very expensive and easily damaged, and it is also easily possible that the fault is in the electrical equipment supporting the HID units, rather than the bulbs themselves.

It is recommended that you use a local auto electrical technician to

If your car has very small headlights within the headlight housing, they are likely to be HID units, as here (your handbook will confirm).

investigate any problems with HID headlights.

Removing the old bulb (non-HID)
• Open the bonnet (hood) and locate the rear of the headlight unit.
• Open the headlight bulb access panel (if fitted), as shown overleaf It may be held by:
1) A spring clip that goes across the back of the panel – the clip is pulled up from the back of the panel thereby allowing the panel to be removed.
2) A plastic clip that needs to be pushed down to release the back panel.
3) A plug in a rubber holder.
• Locate the rear of the bulb that needs replacing and remove its wiring connector – pull the connector off, don't try to remove it by pulling the wires; also try not to twist the connector as you pull it.
   Note: The connector may have two or three wires attached to it, depending on the bulb type (ie: full beam and dipped beam in one bulb or two separate bulbs).
• The bulb itself is held in place by a spring clip over the back, which has one

An electrical danger sticker like this on the back of the headlight unit indicates that HID bulbs are employed.

Opening the headlight access panel at the back of the headlight.

Fig 151. Close-up of a typical wire clip bulb holder. To release the bulb the non-pivoting end of the clip is pushed inward and then slid to the left to release the clip and the bulb.

Removing the bulb's wiring connector by pulling it off the rear of the bulb.

or two small lugs (generally at the top). Push the two lugs together, or push the single lug to one side, and slightly forwards, to release the spring clip so that it comes away from the back of the bulb – the clip will swivel to the side or downward so that the bulb can be removed through the back of the headlight unit.
• Take out the bulb, holding it, if possible, the way it came out of the unit, as this gives you an idea of how to correctly seat the new bulb.

Fig 152. Removing the bulb whilst keeping it in the same orientation.

• Still holding the bulb as you removed it, note its orientation and examine the base closely – there will be indentations and/or mounting lugs on the bulb fitting that you'll have to locate in the same positions to correctly fit the new bulb

Fitting the new bulb (non-HID)
• Take the new bulb from its packaging. **Note:** Do not touch the glass with your fingers (the natural oils in your skin will burn onto the lamp glass when it's first used and reduce brightness. If there isn't a piece of foam around the bulb, handle it with a double layer of tissue.
• Fit the new bulb into its recess in the same orientation as the old bulb.
• Bring the spring clip over the back of the bulb, ensuring that both the clip and bulb are seated correctly; the holding clip will clip into the correct position when pushed forward against the back of the bulb.
• Reattach the wiring connector and test the bulb.
• Replace the panel and fit the securing clip over the back of it.
• Check that the access panel is secure, and close the bonnet.

Fig 153. The base of the bulb shows the spade-type terminals which slot into the connector.

If your car has separate high and low beam bulbs, they can either both be found in the same unit or in separate units. The method for accessing and removing them is usually the same as previously described.

Side lights & front turn indicators
These lights can be in the same cluster or in separate ones, and the bulbs usually push and twist-fit into a rubber/plastic mount.

Some cars will have bulb holders at the rear of the light cluster. To change a bulb in this type of fitting, push in the holder slightly and twist anti-clockwise to remove holder and bulb as one. Push the bulb into the holder and twist to remove it. Replace the bulb with a new one of the same type and wattage, and refit.

Sometimes side lights and/or turn indicator bulbs can be accessed either from the front by undoing the screw or screws retaining the lens, or from the rear, which may give direct access to the holder itself, in which case you simply twist the bulbs anti-clockwise to remove.

Rear light clusters
It's imperative that bulbs in rear light clusters are replaced like-for-like, as each will have a certain wattage, depending on its purpose. You will find the wattage marked on the old bulb or, if in doubt, in the handbook.

Access to the rear of the cluster is normally via a panel inside the rear of the car, or by removing the complete light cluster from the outside of the car.

The access panel may be held closed by clips, screws or even velcro. Once you have access to the bulbs or bulb holders, push the relevant holder in slightly and twist anti-clockwise to remove it – the bulb and holder come out as one. Push the bulb into the holder and twist to remove it. If there are no holders simply push and twist the bulbs to remove.

High-level brake lights
Access is generally by removing a small panel directly behind the unit, or the lens is removed by undoing two screws from the outside.

These lights are normally formed from a number of LEDs. Depending on the manufacturer, these can either be changed one LED at a time, or only as a whole new unit.

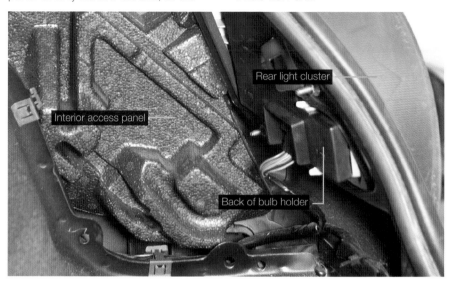

Access to the bulbs in this typical rear light cluster is from the interior luggage area. The panel inside the car is pulled back to reveal the back of the bulb holder.

The bulb holder is pulled away from the rear light cluster, bringing the bulbs with it so that one or more can be replaced.

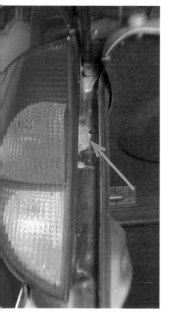

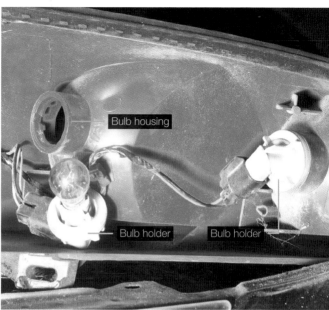

Bulb housing

Bulb holder

Bulb holder

This typical rear light cluster is released from the car's body as a complete unit by undoing a single retaining screw (arrowed). This done, the rear of the unit can be accessed as shown in the next photo.

The back of the cluster reveals the bulb holders. The bulb holder/bulb to the left has been removed from the bulb housing by twisting the holder anti-clockwise.

A typical high-level brake light with two external fixing screws.

six
Wheels/tyres

You do not need any mechanical skills to look after your tyres, and doing so will save you time and money, prevent accidents, and even save a life – maybe yours.

Preventing loss of wheel trims

If you have wheel trims and are concerned about losing them, a simple fix will prevent this: use 'cable ties' to fix the wheel trim to the steel wheel behind it.

Fitting cable ties
• From the front, feed the cable tie through the wheel trim and steel wheel.
• Place your hand around the back of the wheel, and feed the cable tie through the next available hole so it comes out the front.
• Check that the cable tie is not hooked around any hoses or cables behind the wheel.
• Hook the cable tie into itself (at the end) and pull it tight.

• Your wheel trim should now be secured in place.

Cable tie tips
• If you do use cable ties to keep your wheel trims secure, consider what to do when you need to take them off. By design, once a cable tie is in place it cannot be unfastened or removed by hand, so keep a blade or a pair of scissors in the car so that you can cut the cable tie if you need to change the wheel/tyre. Also, keep a few spare cable ties in the car so you can re-secure the wheel trims afterward.
• Purchase quite long cable ties as this will make it easier to fit them, then trim the ends with scissors when fitted.

Checking tyre pressure

Correct tyre pressures are important for many reasons: reducing tyre wear; maintaining fuel efficiency; road grip,

Cable tie for securing wheel trims.

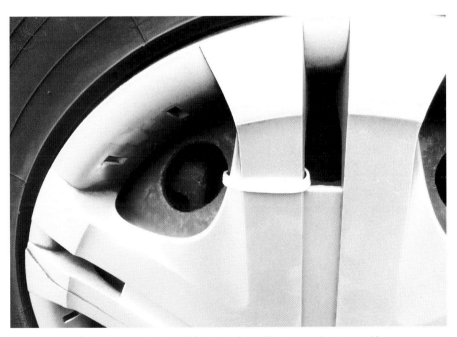

Cable tie securing wheel trim to steel rim. (Courtesy carbasics.co.uk)

and preventing blowouts. Keeping an eye on the tyre pressures can help identify slow punctures before you end up stranded with a flat tyre, or having to change a tyre.

Check the tyres at the fuel station using one of the forecourt air compressors, or get your own tyre pressure gauge or air compressor to use at home. Check tyre pressures at least once a month.

The following method assumes you are using a manual or digital tyre pressure gauge.

Digital tyre pressure gauge.

How to check tyre pressures
• Remove the dust cap from the tyre valve: they unscrew anti-clockwise.
• If you are using a tyre pressure gauge, push the gauge firmly onto the end of the valve and it should register existing tyre pressure.
• Check the tyre pressure against the specific pressures for your car and add/release pressure as required.
• Refit the dust cap onto the tyre valve.
• Repeat this process for the remaining tyres.

What air pressure is correct?
Tyre pressure information will be in your car's user manual, as well as on the car's information plate, most commonly found on the inside of one of the door sills or on the inside of the fuel filler cap. There are also websites that can tell you the correct tyre pressures for your car.

If you have a tyre that loses pressure on a regular basis, it probably has a slow puncture, a faulty valve or a bad seal around the wheel rim. You will need to take this to a tyre shop as soon as possible to get it checked out.

Tyre pressure tips
• Get yourself a tyre inflator or air compressor for checking and inflating tyres at home. Alternatively, consider purchasing a battery booster that incorporates a tyre inflator: see chapter 4: "Using a battery booster."
• Keep a can of emergency puncture repair foam in your car; see "How to fix a tyre puncture."

1	RECOMMENDED INFLATION PRESSURE – COLD,					

RIM SIZE	TIRE SIZE	PRESSURE, kPa(PSI)			
		UP TO 2 PERSONS		UP TO MAX. LOAD	
		FRONT	REAR	FRONT	REAR
4.0 BX13	155/70 R13	210 (30)	210 (30)	220 (32)	220 (32)
4.5 JX13					
5.0 JX14	165/60 R14				
5.5 JX15	175/50 R15				
4.0 TX14	T105/70 D14	420 (60)	420 (60)	420 (60)	420 (60)

THE TIRES FITTED TO THIS VEHICLE SHALL HAVE A MAX. LOAD RATING NOT LESS THAN 387Kg, OR A LOAD INDEX OF 75 AND A SPEED CATEGORY NOT LESS THAN T.

Information plate inside door opening containing tyre pressures.

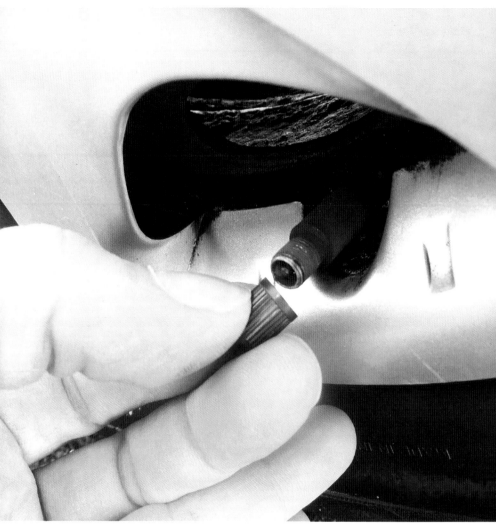

Removing dust cap to check tyre pressures or to apply emergency sealant.

How to fix a tyre puncture

Most small punctures or air leaks can be fixed with emergency sealant/foam that is sprayed from a can into the tyre via the valve to temporarily seal the puncture. This emergency tyre repair solution is suitable for small punctures caused by, say, a screw or a nail.

Before using any sealant, however, read the section at the end of this chapter on Tyre Pressure Monitoring Systems (TPMS).

How to use tyre sealant
Follow the manufacturer's instructions on how to use it, but the following is a brief guide:

- Ensure that you are not in any danger from passing traffic.
- Unscrew the dust cap from the tyre valve.
- Thoroughly shake the can of tyre weld.
- Attach the can to the tyre valve (screw on).
- With the can upside down, press and hold the button.
- You should see the foam going through the clear tube into the tyre.
- It may take a few minutes but make sure that all of the foam has been dispensed.
- When finished refit the tyre valve dust cap.

When you first move the car after using tyre weld, drive slowly so that, as the wheel rotates, the foam is fully dispersed around the inside of the tyre to ensure the puncture is sealed.

The car should now be ok to drive until you get the tyre replaced/repaired (as soon as you can).

Tyre sealant tips
- Do not treat tyre sealant as a permanent fix for any puncture; it is a temporary repair and you must get the tyre changed as soon as you can.
- Once the tyre sealant has stopped the leak don't attempt to remove anything that is sticking out of the tyre, such as a nail or screw, as it will probably start to leak again.

TPMS: a warning
Note! If your vehicle is fitted with a Tyre Pressure Monitoring System (TPMS), be aware that using any kind of tyre sealant will damage the TPMS valve located inside the tyre, and it will have to be replaced. You may feel that this is a worthwhile expense in order to avoid being stranded, but bear in mind this additional cost.

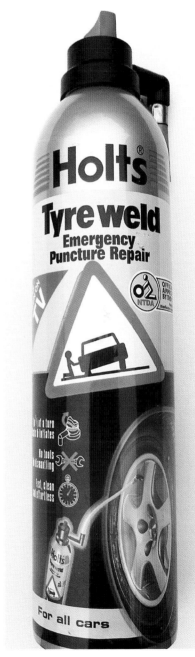

Typical emergency sealant for repairing tyre punctures.

Emergency puncture sealant can tube being screwed on to tyre valve.

Sealant foam about to be pumped into punctured tyre.

seven
Exhaust

The exhaust system sits under the car, subjected to heat, cold, rain, snow, ice, grit, etc. It's not surprising, then, that, over time, parts will rot and deteriorate.

A hole in your exhaust, however, may not necessarily mean replacement, as small holes can be easily repaired at home, using products designed for DIY repair. These make a good, low cost repair, and are easy to use.

If you don't repair exhaust holes as they appear, they will quickly get worse, possibly resulting in the need for a replacement unit. A holed exhaust will not just noisy but will also affect fuel economy.

Holed exhaust pipe, showing soot. (Courtesy carbasics.co.uk)

Exhaust putty for repairing small exhaust holes.

Warning – do not work on a hot exhaust as you risk being burnt. Always let the exhaust cool sufficiently before starting work.

Repairing a hole in the exhaust

Identify where the hole is in your exhaust by the build-up of soot around the area.

The location and/or size of the hole will dictate the type of product – exhaust putty or exhaust wrap – you use to undertake the repair. Exhaust putty is normally used on smaller holes, or in areas where exhaust bandage cannot be fixed, such as in a corner. Exhaust bandage is normally used in easy to access flat areas.

Both products will come with instructions for how to use, but the following is a brief guide, although always read the manufacturer's instructions as they do vary: for example, the Holt exhaust putty instructions recommend applying it to a warm exhaust and moistening the area to give the best result.

Using exhaust putty
• Clean any dirt, soot and rust from the area around the hole with a wire brush.
• Take some of the putty out of the can, and spread it over the hole using a knife or gloved thumb.
• Make sure you press it firmly into the hole and smooth out from the centre.
• Allow to dry and harden.

Using exhaust bandage
Usually the kit will include a strip of foil, securing wire and repair bandage.
Follow the manufacturer's

instructions should they differ from the following brief guide:

• Clean off any dirt, soot and rust from the area around the hole with a wire brush.
• Use some of the foil supplied and fit it over the hole to act as a heat shield.
• Cut off a suitable length of repair bandage, and moisten it so that it becomes flexible.
• Wrap the bandage around the exhaust, pulling it tight and overlapping it sufficiently as you wrap.
• Use the securing wire supplied to hold the bandage in place.
• You should now allow the repair bandage to dry out and give a good repair. Although the heat from the exhaust will help to dry out the bandage, vibration from it can affect the quality of the repair (follow the manufacturer's instructions in this regard).

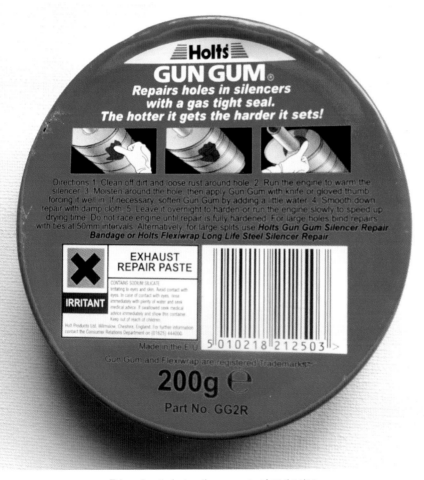

Exhaust putty instructions on rear of packaging.

Exhaust bandage for repairing exhaust holes.

Exhaust putty being applied over hole. (Courtesy carbasics.co.uk)

Exhaust bandage being applied over putty repair. (Courtesy carbasics.co.uk)

eight
Interior

Door panels

How to remove a door panel
Door panels are not as difficult to remove/refit as you may think, as they are usually held in place via a series of screws and door panel clips.

This chapter will also tell you how to repair loose door or interior panels by replacing missing/broken clips.

Door panel clips are designed to press in and out of the metalwork of the car, and door panels can be removed without specialist tools.

Car manufacturers put their cars together in different ways, so the following is general guidance only. Tools you may need are: long, flat-blade screwdriver, cross-head screwdriver, Torx bit set ... and a cutlery fork!

Looking at a door panel, you'll see that all of the fixings holding it in place are hidden, for cosmetic reasons. Removing a panel is best done as a two-part process: removing the door furniture (door handle, etc) first, and secondly the panel itself.

Starting with the door handle, the screws holding it in place will either be on the underside of the handle or hidden behind a cover, which can be removed with the help of a small screwdriver.

Any switches (such as for electric windows) will have a plug on the underside that will simply pull off. If your door panel has a storage pocket at the bottom, this can normally be unscrewed.

If your car has manual windows, look for a circular cover, behind which will be the fixing holding the handle in place. Then pull off the winding handle.

Removing the door panel itself, with the door wide open, start from the bottom corner furthest from the door hinges and, using your long screwdriver, gently prise the door panel away.

The closer you can get the screwdriver to the door panel clips

Plastic door panel clip.

Gently loosening door panel clips with screwdriver.

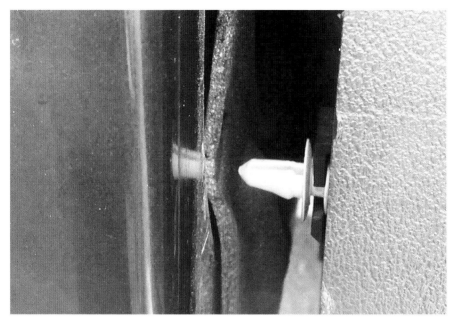

View of released plastic clip behind door panel.

Removing door panel clip with cutlery fork. (Courtesy carbasics.co.uk)

Refitting the door panel: firmly push with fingers/palm to refix door panel clips.

when doing this, the easier it will be to release the panel, minimising risk of damage.

Typically, door panel clips are found at the corners of the panel, and along any long edges. Work your way around the panel until all the clips have been released.

The panel should now lift off, but check for any missed clips if it doesn't.

How to refit a door panel
Offer up the door panel and align the panel clips with the relevant holes. Work around the panel, pressing the door panel clips into place.

Now refit the remaining plastic parts such as the lower storage pocket and door handle. Remember to re-attach any electrical wiring plugs.

Door panel removal tips
• Take your time when working on door panels, and ensure that you have removed all of the fixings before trying to lift away the panel.
• If any of the door panel clips are difficult to remove or remain in the door when the panel is removed, they can sometimes be removed using a cutlery fork.
• If any of your door panel clips break, these are readily available from your local car spares shop or online. Consider buying some spare clips before you start work on your door panels.

Refitting a rear view mirror

Rear view mirrors are prone to getting knocked from the windscreen, especially if your car is quite old and the mirror has been in place for some time.

Refitting an interior mirror is not a difficult job, and you won't need any

specialist tools to do it, although don't imagine that a dab of superglue will hold it in place for very long.

For the best chance of a long term repair, follow the guidance in this section, along with any instructions in the repair kit you purchase. Your local car parts shop will have interior mirror repair kits, but ensure that the kit is in date, and is a reputable brand. Cutting corners and buying a cheap repair kit will not result in a good, long-term repair.

Separating the mirror
Your rear view mirror comprises two parts, connected via a ball joint. One part houses the mirror glass, and the other is the piece that attaches to the windscreen (the mirror base). The first task is to separate these two parts, otherwise the mirror will be too heavy, and will drop off before the adhesive has had chance to work. The two parts usually just prise apart, and press back together with a little effort.

Refixing the mirror base
You should follow the manufacturer's instructions exactly, although the following is a brief guide:

• Sand both the mirror base and the windscreen button (metal disc on windscreen) so that they are completely smooth (rough surfaces will prevent the glue making a strong join).
• Once both surfaces completely smooth, remove any dust and dirt from them.
• Apply the glue to one or both surfaces (according to manufacturer's instructions), press the two parts together, and hold in place.
• Hold the mirror base to the windscreen button (metal disc on windscreen) for as long as the instructions say to do.

• Allow the glue to set overnight before refitting the mirror (see below).

Refitting the mirror
After allowing sufficient time for the glue to set, you can refit the mirror to the base that is now glued to the windscreen. Take care not to break off the mirror base from the windscreen. Try holding the base in one hand whilst pressing the mirror on with the other.

Remember to refit any electrical wiring that goes to the interior mirror.

The repair should now be complete.

Tips for refitting interior mirrors
• The cleaner and smoother the two surfaces are, the better the chance of them staying glued together.
• When glueing the mirror base to the windscreen button (metal disc on windscreen), hold them together for as long as you can: the longer you do this, the better the repair.
• Do not drive the car straight away as the vibration will weaken the joint.

Showing rear of interior mirror: two components separate at ball joint.

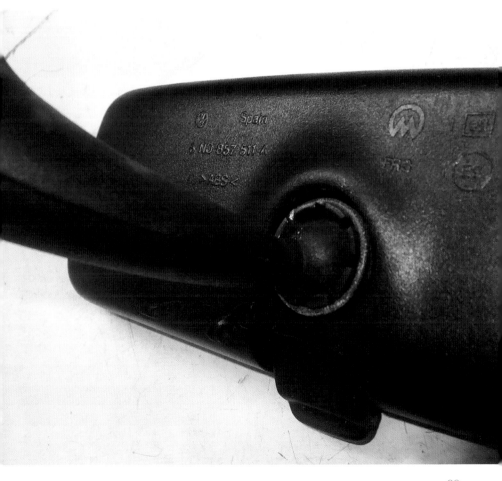

nine

Bodywork

You don't need to take your car to the bodyshop in order to keep it looking good.

Replacing door mirror glass

If the glass in the door mirror gets broken, there is a quick and easy fix. Most car parts shops sell replacement door mirror glass that sticks directly over the broken glass, and does not require you to dismantle the mirror. You can also buy replacement mirror glass online.

The replacement mirror glass you purchase will be the right size and shape for your vehicle and, when fitted correctly, will act as a permanent repair that is significantly cheaper than replacing the entire door mirror assembly.

Fitting self-adhesive mirror glass
Designed to stick onto the broken mirror glass, the following is a brief guide:
• Remove any loose pieces of broken

mirror glass (those that are no longer attached).
• Unpack the replacement mirror glass
• Remove the paper backing from the mirror glass.
• Align the new mirror glass over the broken glass.
• When in the correct position, press the mirror glass into place over the existing broken pieces, making sure you apply pressure across the entire surface so that it sticks securely in place, but taking care not to injure yourself on the broken pieces.
• Give your replacement mirror glass a good clean to remove finger marks and smears.

Tips for fitting mirror glass
• If you can't find exactly the right mirror glass for your car, there is a simple alternative. Make a cardboard template of your existing mirror glass and take it to the nearest auto spares shop (remember to mark which is

Broken door mirror glass can be quickly and easily repaired.

the front and which side of the car it comes from). You should be able to buy mirror glass that is either universal, or very similar in shape and size to your template.

- Ensure you purchase the right mirror as driver and passenger sides are different.
- Note! The adhesive backing on the replacement glass is very strong: be sure to fit it in the right place first time, you won't be able to take it off to refit it.

Warning! Take care not to cut yourself on the broken mirror parts.

Removing tar spots

Removing tar spots from paintwork is easier than you think, using the following useful and very cheap fix.

WD-40 spray is an excellent,

all-purpose product to keep around the house: it lubricates, penetrates, displaces water, and cleans. It also works very well for removing tar from paintwork.

A little sprayed on the affected area should break down the tar so that it can be wiped off with a cloth, without causing any reaction or marking of the paintwork, although you should always clean the area with a clean cloth straight after.

Paintwork restoring products such as T-cut® are also good at removing tar spots (see Removing small scratches and marks, overleaf).

Warning – when using WD-40 or similar on or near wheels, ensure it does not get on brake discs or pads, as this will affect braking performance. Apply the product sparingly to a cloth, and use to remove tar spots.

WD-40 for cleaning tar spots from bodywork.

Paint restorer/scratch remover for removing small bodywork scratches.

Removing small scratches and marks

Small scratches or marks in your paint may not mean a trip to a bodyshop for an expensive repair, as many scratches can be removed at very little cost using scratch remover or paint restorer products: essentially very mild abrasive liquids that will restore paintwork to original condition. T-cut® and Meguiars scratchX® are paintwork restorers that can be used all over, as well as on smaller areas.

Using scratch remover liquids

Try not to get the liquid on rubber parts around windows and plastics. If you do, wipe off before it dries or else it will leave marks that can be difficult to remove later.

Follow the manufacturer's instructions, and use the following as a brief guide:

• Before using the scratch remover, wash the area to remove any debris that could cause more scratches.

• Apply liquid to a clean, lint-free cloth.

• Rub the liquid over the scratched area using small, circular movements.

• The scratch should gradually reduce and eventually disappear.

Tips for using scratch remover

• For the best results apply to small areas and buff off immediately with a clean, soft cloth.

• Certain scratch removers are available in colours to match your car's paintwork, and these may give an even better result.

Applying scratch remover using lint-free cloth.

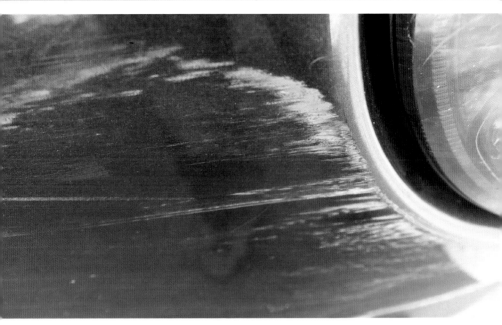

Bodywork mark before using scratch remover. (Courtesy carbasics.co.uk)

Bodywork after using scratch remover. (Courtesy carbasics.co.uk)

• Scratch removers are useful for removing the adhesive when badges and graphics have been taken off.

• Take care when using scratch remover liquids near the edges of bodywork as too much or too hard rubbing may result in removing paint.

• Scratch removers cannot rectify deep scratches: a different product is required for this (see "Repairing larger scratches").

Repairing larger scratches

A deep scratch would be one that has removed the paintwork right down to the metal primer or metal itself, but it may still be possible to repair bodywork at home using a touch-up pen, designed to exactly match the colour of your car's paintwork.

Establishing your car's paint code
You will need to find the paint code for your car so that you can match the paint colour. A plate/label on your car –

typically found in the engine bay area or inside one of the doors – will have the details of your car's paint code.

If you can't find the plate with your car's colour code information, search on the internet to determine the location.

How to use a touch-up pen
Follow the manufacturer's instructions: the following is a brief guide:

• Clean the scratch and surrounding area, removing any wax or grease.

• Thoroughly shake the touch-up pen to mix the paint.

• Apply the colour in thin layers using the pen or paint brush supplied. Don't try and cover the scratch with one coat.

• Allow the paint to dry thoroughly

• If supplied, apply the top coat and allow to dry.

Touch-up pen tips
• To get a good quality repair, it will be worth paying a little extra for a good quality product.

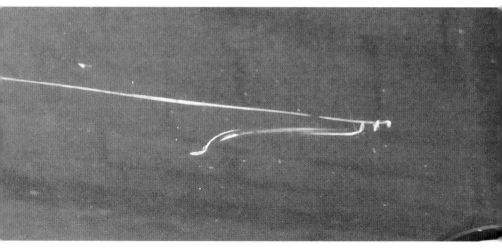

Deep scratch showing undercoat.

ISBN: 978-1-845845-19-3
Paperback • 21x14.8cm
£12.99* UK/$24.95* USA
128 pages • 137 colour pictures

ISBN: 978-1-845844-74-5
Paperback • 21x14.8cm
£9.99* UK/$19.95* USA
80 pages • 99 colour pictures

ISBN: 978-1-845844-50-9
Paperback • 21x14.8cm
£9.99* UK/$19.95* USA
96 pages • 136 colour pictures

ISBN: 978-1-845844-49-3
Paperback • 21x14.8cm
£9.99* UK/$19.95* USA
80 pages • 109 colour and
b&w pictures

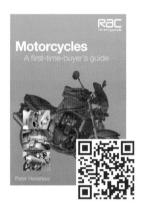

ISBN: 978-1-845844-95-0
Paperback • 21x14.8cm
£9.99* UK/$19.95* USA
80 pages • 95 colour pictures

ISBN: 978-1-845845-32-2
Paperback • 21x14.8cm
£9.99* UK/$19.95* USA
80 pages • 100 pictures

For more info on Veloce titles, visit our website at www.veloce.co.uk
email: info@veloce.co.uk • Tel: +44(0)1305 260068
* prices subject to change, p&p extra

ISBN: 978-1-845843-96-0
Paperback • 21x14.8cm
£9.99* UK/$19.95* USA
96 pages • 177 colour pictures

ISBN: 978-1-845843-88-5
Paperback • 21x14.8cm
£9.99* UK/$19.95* USA
80 pages • 115 colour pictures

ISBN: 978-1-845843-90-8
Paperback • 21x14.8cm
£12.99* UK/$24.95* USA
104 pages • 92 colour and
b&w pictures

ISBN: 978-1-845840-95-2
Paperback • 21x14.8cm
£9.99* UK/$19.95* USA
80 pages • 89 colour pictures

ISBN: 978-1-845844-77-6
Paperback • 21x14.8cm
£6.99* UK/$11.99* USA
64 pages • 97 colour pictures

ISBN: 978-1-845844-94-3
Paperback • 21x14.8cm
£9.99* UK/$19.99* USA
80 pages • 86 colour pictures

For more info on Veloce titles, visit our website at www.veloce.co.uk
email: info@veloce.co.uk • Tel: +44(0)1305 260068
* prices subject to change, p&p extra

E-Books from Veloce Publishing
WWW.VELOCE.CO.UK

E-Books available for your E-reader, tablet, smart phone, iPod and desktop computer.

Available on all the major E-Book marketplaces.

For more info on Veloce titles, visit our website at www.veloce.co.uk
email: info@veloce.co.uk • Tel: +44(0)1305 260068
* prices subject to change, p&p extra

Index